Pay With Paper

A beginner's guide to learn the art of couponing!

Jennifer Cuartas

Table of Contents

Chapter 1

My story & I'm sticking to it!

Everyone who coupons has a reason they chose to begin couponing. For many, the economy has condensed their pocketbook. For others, they may simply like the idea of not having to pay full price for something that they don't have to. Whatever your reason or whether you are looking to save a little; or to the extreme, you are sure to find very helpful information in the following chapters to develop enough of an understanding to accomplish your savings goals. I will tell you up front that I do not claim to be an expert in any way. Everything I have learned in regards to couponing I have done so by trial and error. The tips and techniques that I have included for you, I use personally to achieve savings of 50% to 90% each time I buy groceries so I know first-hand that they work!

My personal coupon journey started the minute that I learned of the amazing opportunity of "paying for my groceries with paper", as I like to refer to it. I was at a point where I was barely keeping my kids fed and my husband and I were basically alternating which meals we would skip. On average we ate just one meal a day and when we would eat it was just enough to satisfy the hunger pain. Unfortunately, for us, this scenario was just going to keep getting worse. We had to find a way to fix the problem. However, the real problem for me was that this was all new for me and I did not know where to begin. The short story is that my 15 month old daughter woke up sick one morning and life immediately and drastically changed for us. I had to learn pretty quickly how to redirect our spending in order to cover our bills, her medical expenses, travel to children's hospitals out of town, and still be able to put food on the table. After months and months of testing and learning that this would be a lifetime ordeal for her was shocking to our family. I realized that I needed to now find a long term solution. With coupons, I have been able to do that!

Prior to this new scenario I had been presented with, I had only used coupons here and there as I would come across one for something I was going to buy. I was aware of the concept that coupons could save a few cents on each item, but I was blind to the amazing and very real possibilities of saving hundreds of dollars per month. The very second that I found out there are people who had mastered the art of couponing and were using them to save hundreds of dollars per shopping trip, that really intrigued me to explore this a bit further. I knew that for me, this was a solution to a very large problem if I could learn how to do it myself.

How I was introduced to the power of using coupons, was when I had come across a picture of friends shopping receipts that she posted online to show all of her friends what an awesome time she had shopping. She purchased 200 boxes of cereal for less than five dollars. I was shocked. Then I cried. She later posts online that she went to another store on the same day and scores toiletries, diapers and cleaners for less than $20. All I could think as I am looking at the pictures of her products and receipts was how is this possible? The town we lived in is really small. We shopped at the same stores. As a matter of fact, I shopped at the very same grocery store several times per week and NEVER did I see a sale *that* good! I always *tried* to be a savvy shopper, looked for sales, used the few coupons I always seemed to come across in the paper, and always took my time to shop for the best deals. There had to be something I was missing. All I could think about in the following days is what was I doing wrong? Why was I not able to get my groceries for these rock bottom prices? I literally went through a roller coaster of emotion beating myself up because of my own *need* to save like she had saved.

Needless to say, I immediately took it upon myself to look into every aspect of this new phenomenon! Learning to coupon became very high up on my agenda of things to do. Let's just say that I am a strong believer that if one person is capable of achieving something, aside from natural born talent, anyone can duplicate it. Keeping in mind that with anything new you encounter, there is a learning curve... I was ready to learn. I looked in sales ads. I looked in the newspaper for coupons. I started researching online for all the information I could drum up. I signed up for mailing lists. I was able to find a limited amount of information but the problem is none of the "how-to" type sites went into enough detail to save more than just a few dollars per trip.

I broke down and emailed my friend and asked her if she could tell me how she was able to score such a find. Her response was almost depressing. All she replied with: *by using coupons and sales.* Really? Three words were *all* I got! *Huh?* I asked a few more questions in my response to her inadequate answer to probe her for details. She would not budge. Seriously? An explanation was what I was expecting. I was so confused, because to me, I believe that if you find a great deal, you share it! Hence, this is the reason for me sharing with all of you in this book!

After several conversations on the topic she never divulged the information which thrust me into a roller coaster ride of a mission trying to sort the dos and don'ts as I curb the urge to learn couponing. I did not understand the lingo so reading the few coupon blogs that existed was like speaking to me in gibberish. I made embarrassing mistakes. I held up lines during the checkout process. I missed out on sales because I was not properly organized. Right as I am about to give up, I score my first free haul, six FREE toothbrushes. Well, I actually paid .26 for tax. But it was FREE! (Insert happy dance here) Funny thing is, I didn't need any toothbrushes and I didn't care! Once I got to my vehicle and started up the car, I reacted as if I had won the lottery! It wasn't so much the toothbrushes, rather the satisfaction that I reached my goal! I had finally figured this thing out! It felt so good. Before I knew it, couponing had become almost an obsession. It was like a game almost. My 11 year old son and I would try to guess how much money we would save and who ever got the closest would have to make sandwiches when we got home.

Then I was ready to push the envelope a bit! That is when I learned the hard way that you better understand the stores policies before you shop. I was going in for my largest haul up to this point. I was buying 30 jars of mayonnaise and 50 condensed milks. I get to the counter, I was nervous and excited at the same time and then it happens. I had misunderstood the coupon lingo. To say that I was embarrassed is an understatement. I had to put all of that stuff back on the shelves. I got the wrong sizes, I had the wrong coupons and I wanted to crawl into a hole. I went home and decided that I had enough, bagged up my coupons and plopped them into the recycle bin. Later to only take them out and start all over again as I did not have another solution to overcome our issue with paying for groceries! This time I was determined to get it right and I suppose I did because here I am today, saving 50% on a bad week and teaching others how to do the same! Who would have thought?

My greatest advice is to not get frustrated. Do not give up. It takes a few weeks to get acclimated to "think like a couponer". It also takes time to build up your arsenal of coupons and the knowledge to combine those coupons with the weekly retail deals and maximize your savings. If you stick with it, I promise you it will pay off in the end. The amount you save will ultimately be determined by the amount of time and effort you put into it but you have a huge advantage that I didn't! You have this book! In the following chapters, I have included much of the information that was not readily available to me when I started couponing. Information that can make or break you as an efficient couponer! Knowledge is power so I hope that you use what you learn here and are able to take from it enough knowledge to get you saving amounts you never dreamed possible.

Chapter 2

Understanding the Lingo

The first step to learning how to use coupons to save upwards of 50% to 70% of your grocery bill is to learn the lingo. It will be very important in regards to finding the deals and when you do, avoiding any embarrassing moments.

You may be familiar some of these already. However, for those terms that are new to you, I have outlined them in alphabetical order for quick reference. You are likely to see these on coupon sites, coupon related blogs, in store policies, sales ads and even on coupons themselves. It is important to understand each of their meaning to ensure you are utilizing your coupons correctly ultimately maximizing your bottom line.

$$/$$ - $ off when you spend $ amount. Example: $10/$50 are $10 off your purchase when you spend $50. (Check your store policy to see if they state whether the amount has to be before or after coupons to apply.)

$/# - $ off for every # you buy. Example: $5/2 would mean that you get $5 off every 2 that you buy.

B1G1 - Buy One Get One Free (B1G2 is Buy One Get Two Free etc.)

Blinkie - A coupon that prints out of a dispenser machine located with the product associated with that particular coupon.

BOGO - Buy One Get One Free

Bricks - "Bricks" coupons are internet printable coupons. If you print a "bricks" coupon, you will know based on a picture of a computer/printer with a small blinking dot as it sends the information to your printer. You can normally only print 1 of these coupons. However if you hit your back button 3 times after it is sent to the printer it will generally print a second copy of the coupon for you. If you want additional copies then you will need to use another computer.

CAT - See Catalina.

Catalina - Also referred to as CAT. A coupon that prints out at the register that is either $$ off your next purchase or $$ off a certain product. You typically have to use them at the store they printed, but some stores will take "competitor's" coupons.

Closeouts - Typically greatly reduced items that the store does not plan on re-stocking.

Competitors - Competitor coupons are normally accepted to match prices of local "related chains." For example, Wal-Mart may take Target coupons, or CVS may take Walgreen's store coupons. Always check with each store to determine which store chains they consider to be a competitor as it varies by each demographic.

Coupon Policy - Each store has a coupon policy. The policy stipulates what their procedure is in regards to using coupons. This policy will advise if they accept competitor coupons, if they allow doubling or stacking, etc. Policies change often and vary from store to store based on manager's discretion. It is important to contact the store you frequent and find out their coupon policy before shop.

Coupon Insert - These are "packets" of coupons found in Sunday papers typically including coupons issued by Smart Source (SS or S), Red Plum (RP) and Proctor & Gamble (PG).

CRT - Cash Register Tape, or your receipt.

Dead - This term is most commonly associated with internet printable coupons that run out of prints or is no longer valid.

DND - Do Not Double. Manufacturers sometimes place a DND at the top of the coupon by the expiration date, meaning that the coupon should not be doubled at the store.

Discontinued - The store does not plan on re-stocking this item.

Double Coupons - Some stores will double a coupon's value, up to a certain denomination. Example, if you have a $1 off coupon, they will double the coupon making it worth $2 off. This is an important policy to become familiar with at your local stores. Not all stores or states allow coupons to be doubled. In some occasions, the store may also set a maximum value limit. In other words, you have a coupon for $1, they match it up to .50 making your coupon savings $1.50.

ECB - Extra Care Bucks. Exclusive to CVS. You earn ECB by purchasing certain items listed with the ECB logo in the weekly sales ad. The items vary each week. You purchase one of the items and receive a print out of $$ off of your next purchase. Hint: Break up your transactions in the same shopping trip to maximize your ECB savings!

ES -Easy Saver, Walgreen's rebate booklet. The books are found by their sales ads in the store.

EX or EXP - Expires or Expiration Date

FAR - Free after Rebate (Refer to Rebate for explanation)

FAE - Free after Extra Care Bucks (Refer to ECB or Extra Care Bucks for explanation)

FARR - Free after Register Rewards (Refer to RR or Register Rewards for explanation)

GM - General Mills Coupon Insert. Located in the Sunday paper coupon inserts.

HOT - Hot Deal or Coupon, a deal or coupon that is valid for a short time or that will not last long.

Inserts - These are "packets" of coupons found in Sunday papers and also sometimes in the ads mailed to you during the week in other local publications. These are typically sent out by Smart Source (SS or S), Red Plum

(RP) and Proctor & Gamble (PG). Sometimes General Mills (GM) or local stores.

Internet Printable - A coupon that can be printed online.

IP - Internet Printable Coupon. Also referred to as "printable."

IVC - Instant Value Coupon. These are Walgreen's store coupons and are located in their weekly sales ads.

MFR - Manufacturer coupon

MIR - Mail In Rebate. These can be in the form of either checks or coupons that the manufacturers will send you if you meet the requirements on the rebate form.

MQ - Manufacturer Coupon

NED - No Expiration Date, a coupon that has no expiration date.

NT WT - Net Weight, in reference to coupons that stipulate that you must purchase a product with a specific net weight in order to utilize the coupon.

OOP - Out-of-Pocket. The amount of money spent after all coupons and discounts have been applied.

OOS - Out-of-Stock. The store is temporarily out of an item but plans on getting in more inventory. When this occurs, ask about a raincheck.

OTC - Over the counter medication.

OYNO - On Your Next Order.

OYNP - On Your Next Purchase.

Peelie - Coupons found on products in the store. Make sure to pull them off right away and include them in your coupons during check out.

PG or P&G = Proctor & Gamble. Included in the Sunday coupon "packet".

Pintables - Coupons that can be printed off the internet.

POP – Proof of purchase. (Refer to MIR)

Q - Coupon

RC or Rain check - Get this from customer service when a store has an item on sale and it is out-of-stock.

RP - Red Plum. This is a coupon insert that you'll either find in your Sunday paper in the coupon "packet" or sometimes in the mail.

Register Rewards - Exclusive to Walgreen's. They work like cash on your next order. (Some restrictions do apply)

RR - Refer to Register Rewards.

S or SS - Smart Source. This is a large supplier of coupon. You will find SS coupons in the Sunday paper as well as on their website, www.smartsource.com for printables.

Stacking- Using 1 manufacturer coupon and 1 store coupon on the same product (if store coupon policy allows).

Tear pad – A pad found hanging from a

store shelf or display, normally with the product it is associated with. This could be either coupons or MIR.

Triple Coupons - This is the term used when stores will triple a coupon's value. Example, if you have a $1 off coupon, they'll take $3 off. Check with your stores coupon policy to see if and when they allow this.

UPC - Universal Bar Code. This is the bar code that's scanned on products for pricing/info at the stores. Several companies will ask you to mail these in on rebates.

WAGS - Abbreviation for Walgreen's.

WT - Wine Tag. These coupons are hanging on the top of wine bottles.

WYB - When You Buy.

YMMV - Your Mileage May Vary. This term is used to say that a particular deal worked for one person, but may not work for another. In other words, it may not work at all store locations.

Fun Fact:

The first coupon was created in 1887 by the gentleman that invented the syrup used today in Coca-Cola! It was good for one free Coca-Cola drink at a particular pharmacy. The purpose was to get the product known and to encourage people to buy it... do you think it worked?

Chapter 3

Power of the Policy

You now have touched on what terms and abbreviations are used in the coupon world. The next thing you need to know, and I feel is the most important, is to understand the coupon policies in place at each store you plan to shop.

Obtain a copy of the stores coupon policy by one of the following:
Calling the store directly.
Some corporate stores will email you a copy via request.
Ask for a copy of the policy at the customer service counter.
Publix and a few other retailers post them at the main entrance.

No matter which way you obtain the policy, just obtain it! It will sort out much needed information like which stores they consider to be competitors, if they take competitor coupons, if stacking or doubling is allowed. It will also detail any other pertinent information that will help you along your couponing journey.

```
Important:
If you are going to email the store for
their coupon policy, request they mail you
a "hard copy" of the current policy. In the
event that you find yourself in a situation
where either the cashier or the manager
is not up to speed on their current policy
you will have something tangible to fall
back on. Especially because it will be
addressed directly to you from the
corporate office!!
```

Here are some sample questions of what you may want to ask when inquiring about the coupon policy of your favorite stores!

* What types of coupons do you accept?
* Do you also accept competitor coupons? If so, from which stores?
* Do you double/triple coupons?
* Do you have store coupons? How often do they come out? Where can I get them?

* What is your policy in the event that I have an overage?
* May I stack a manufacturer and a store coupon together?
* Do you limit the amount of coupons/items may be used per transaction?

It is also very important to know what cycles the store sales and ads run in. This will vary by store. Example: Wednesday - Tuesday / Monday - Sunday.

Once you have a good grasp on the policies of the stores you shop, you will be able to use that in conjunction with your coupons to decide how to configure your shopping trip accordingly. This will also help to avoid any uncomfortable or embarrassing situations that may occur during check out. Do not be afraid to split your purchases up into several transactions in the same shopping trip. This may actually help you to save more money. Keep this in mind when shopping at stores like CVS and Walgreens that have rewards programs that allow you to earn "cash off" of your "next" purchase!

Example of CVS shopping trip with ECBs:

Transaction 1:
XYZ item $2.49
Buy 1, get $2.00 ECB... You pay .49!

Transaction 2:
ABC item $1.99
Use $2 ECB from 1st transaction... You pay nothing!

Knowing the store policy will help you score many deals like this when you are buying multiples of items!

Chapter 4

Coupon Resources:

To save with coupons is to have coupons!

I treat coupons as preciously as I do money. Why? The answer is simple! If you had a jar full of quarters, would you throw them away? I didn't think so! Well, in laments terms that is how I view couponing! It actually pains me to see coupons in the trash.

Why? If someone gave you a quarter every day for a year straight, that would be $91.25.

> How I got that figure:
> .25 (a day)
> x 365 (days a year)
> $91.25

Now thinking like a "couponer" you will equate this to a stack of coupons.

Once you start building up your coupon base and begin to match them with the on-going sales, you will see that you can save substantially *every time* you shop because you are not using only one 25 cent coupon each shopping trip as with the example used above, you are going to use 15 or 30 or even more as you develop your system. You will eventually want to get to the point where you save 50% to 90% of your bill! However, just as you cannot spend money you physically do not have, you cannot save money without the coupons. So, the real key to becoming an expert couponer and never miss a deal is to collect as many coupons as you can. You need to have an arsenal of them. This includes having several duplicates of the same coupon. So, where do you get them?

Start with friends and family:

The truth is not everyone sees the value of coupons. Or maybe it is simply that they do not have the knowledge you are learning right now. Whatever the reason, they trash them! Capitalize on that! Remember that each Sunday there is an average of $150 in savings just by simply getting a single newspaper. You have friends and family right now that are throwing away thousands of dollars in the trash and probably do not even know it!

The task: Ask all of your friends and family if they use coupons. The people, who answer "no", see if they mind giving you all of their coupons that come in the mail and/or in the Sunday paper to help get you started. If they answer "yes", you now have a coupon buddy to swap unused coupons with.

Newspaper:

Contact your local newspaper service and purchase multiple Sunday papers. No matter where you live, you are bound to find at least one newspaper that includes Sunday coupons. If you live in an area that has multiple papers you should, in most cases, go with the largest and most popular one as they are more prone to having the largest assortment of coupons.

If you are worried about the cost of the paper in the beginning don't go crazy ordering 20 papers. You can always start small and as you start seeing savings, use that money to add more later. However, I would recommend purchasing at least two papers minimum so that you will have duplicate coupons for the BOGO (buy one, get one) offers.

Local Publications:

I have discovered that there are many small papers as well as local, free papers, forums and small journals or publications now including Smartsource (SS) and Redplum (RP) coupon inserts. The ones I have found are not issued on Sundays, rather more towards the mid-week days. I would recommend contacting these papers and asking what day they come out. Also inquire where you might be able to pick some up and see of they will arrange a way for you to receive multiple copies. Some will do home deliveries or mail outs as well, upon request.

Internet Printable Coupons:

As you know, the internet has ultimately changed the way the world does business. This is not any different when it comes to couponing. There are many websites dedicated to couponing and because of this I would not recommend any site that charges a fee as you can certainly find a printable coupon for free on another site.

There are many worthy coupon sites to choose from. Do a simple search with the word "coupon" and thousands of pages will come up. Here are a few of the sites I use.

- www.smartsource.com
- www.redplum.com
- www.coupons.com
- www.coupons.info
- www.groupon.com
- www.extremefreecoupons.com
- www.couponbug.com
- www.dailygrocerycoupon.com
- www.couponmom.com
- www.coolsavings.com
- www.retailmenot.com

Start by taking a look at these sites, but you will want to search for others as well that fit your specific needs. Make sure to bookmark the ones that you plan on using the most!

> Internet coupons will require you to install coupon printing software on your computer. It is free, however limits you to only print two (2) copies, per computer, of each coupon printed. Hit the "back" button to submit to print a second copy.

Internet coupons really started becoming popular in 1999. Most stores are now accepting printed coupons; however you will want to check with each store to verify their policy.

Blogs:

Blogs are a great way to find not only coupons but also sale match ups, freebies and local deals. The best thing to do is find a blog that is central to your area to follow. You do not want to randomly follow just any blog as the coupon rules may be different, as well as prices, deals and such in the area the blog is being published from.

What I like best about a good coupon blog is that they usually will highlight the best deals from the weekly sales paper from multiple store chains and break down the sale price, which coupons to use, the date they came out as well as the final price you should expect to pay. A good blog will also provide a link to the printable coupons available on said item.

Example of a match up you might find on a blog:

XYZ Juice, 64 oz $3.49
Use $1.00/1 Coupon from SS 1/8
and ZYX Grocery $1.00/1 in store coupon
Final Price: As low as $1.49 each

The best part of following a local blog is that the blogger most likely lives in your area and dedicated their time to finding savings. This means that you will most likely also find local deals that are not advertised in the form of an actual coupon, but are great money saving opportunities.

Be sure to follow the Couponing Divas Blog:
http://couponingdivas.blogspot.com

Social Media:

That's right, I am saying it! Facebook, is yet another awesome place to find fantastic coupons. Facebook is no longer only for communicating with your friends and family. Use the Facebook search bar to look up the pages of your favorite products. You will find that many of them will offer you a printable coupon for clicking the "like" button on their page. After your coupon prints, make sure to hit the "back" button to select to print a second copy. Check the page often for future coupon codes and printables.

Email:

Locate the websites for your favorite food, drink and snack items. Most sites will have a link for you to submit your email address to be put on their mailing lists. You will receive information on new products, but most importantly coupons to use on them!

Before submitting your email to any of the sites, I would recommend taking five minutes to set up a designated email for your new couponing venture.

Here is a list of a few free email services:

- www.yahoo.com
- www.gmail.com
- www.mail.com
- www.hotmail.com
- www.gmx.com
- www.inbox.com

If you put "free email" in your preferred internet search bar you will get many more available services. I do not recommend one over the other. They are all great services! Take a look at each one and choose which you prefer, pick a name and set it up!

You also may want to sign up for "inbox alerts" from other sites that will send you coupons and daily deals.

Mobile Coupons:

Now this is probably the newest of the avenues available to couponers. Mobile coupons are an interesting concept. If you are not one to print, clip and file your coupons this may be a neat paperless option for you. Or, if you have a busy schedule and would like to coupon on the go, this may be something to look into.

Basically what this involves is a website that you will visit either via computer or your smartphone. You will browse through all of the available discounts and coupons. Once you select the ones you would like to take advantage of, a bar code is sent to your phone by the click of a button. You then show the bar code on your phone to the cashier who will then scan it as any other coupon. Presto! The discounts will come off your total!

Here are a few examples of sites that specialize in mobile coupons. Some are free services, some are via membership only. As you should always, make sure you read the FAQs and fine print before engaging in any contract or service.

- www.mobilecoupons.com
- www.coupious.com
- www.cellfire.com
- www.mymobiledeals.com

Smartphone Applications (Apps):

As technology has evolved, so has the way we make use of our cell phones. If you have an app enabled phone there are many apps that you can download and use for free. You will be able to search deals in your immediate area, or a particular store, sales ads, coupon codes and much more. The world of apps has made my couponing task more efficient. It is definitely something to look into and research if you plan to make a real go at couponing.

As you can see, there are many avenues you can take in obtaining the best coupons available and I am sure as technology advances, so will the ways to save. My only recommendation is whether you are new to couponing or an expert; familiarize yourself extensively with which ever vehicles you choose to use to obtain your coupons. Maybe start with one or two and once you are familiar add a third and so on. I am not saying you have to use all of the methods I have demonstrated, but use a few of them to get a good assortment of savings and to see which works best in your lifestyle.

Tip:

Do not throw away coupons for items you think you will never buy or use. Look for deals on these items in which you can get them for free or where overages from these items may be possible. Use the overages to pay for your other items and donate the unwanted goodies to homeless shelters or organization of your choice!

Chapter 5

Coupons not Crimes:

Story of the coupon hoarder!

So now you have some of the basics down and you are ready to start saving money couponing... but at what cost? There is a growing trend and epidemic popping up in cities across America. Stealing coupons! I refer to these thieves as *"Coupon Hoarders"*.

Maybe it is the economy that is driving people to commit crimes for couponing or maybe it is something completely foreign to my mind. Whatever the reason, there is no need for it. There are plenty of legit ways to accommodate your couponing lifestyle which you just learned about in the last chapter.

What is a "coupon hoarder"? In the shortest answer possible, a person that will go to any and all extremes to get EVERY coupon they can possibly get their hands on and don't mind breaking the law in order to do it. They will steal papers out of your driveway, out of local dumpsters, pay for one paper at a newspaper machine and take them ALL! This is a person that has no problem criminally securing coupons.

My encounter with the *coupon hoarder*:
As I am pulling up in front of a newspaper machine I am startled as this blue van pulls in front of me, almost hitting the front of my vehicle. A woman jumps out, runs over to the machine, puts in $2, takes ALL of the papers (maybe 25 or so), jumps back into her van and speeds off before I can blink an eye. Are you kidding me?

If you are new to couponing you may not know that these people exist. You may also not realize the impact that this may have on couponing in the future. Newspapers may eventually stop supplying coupons at all of it means people steal their papers and cut their profits. Cities may ban the use of newspaper machines if it becomes a dangerous event to score a paper. Not to mention that manufacturers may stop printing them or stores may stop taking them all together if it causes issues in their target markets.

I know many people coupon due to the poor state of our economy and I am not convinced it is going to get any better. However, that is no reason to become a criminal in order to coupon. There are plenty of legitimate ways to save money. It is a crime to pay for one paper and take an entire stack. In some states it is considered petty theft; some consider it fraudulent destruction, punishable up to one year in jail and a $4000 fine. If you see someone engaging in this activity, I encourage you to discourage it! In the end, we will all suffer if these people keep committing these crimes!

Fun Fact:
According to NCH Marketing, there were 311 billion coupons distributed in 2009. Americans saved an astounding $3.5 Billion with coupons making it the largest ever recorded in history!

Chapter 6

Organization is Key

Now that you know how to and not to go about building your coupon arsenal, where do you keep the coupons once you get them? The last thing you want is to end up with coupons all over the place. I assure you that you do not want to let these little buggers end up in the kitchen, on your dresser, in your pockets, covering your tables, lining the floor of your car, in your purse and anywhere else they might end up! You also do not want to end up with an enormous stack of Sunday coupon inserts that who knows what coupons they contain! Otherwise, you will end up scurrying about, because you know you saw a coupon for those paper towels or hand soap that is now on sale... and it's, um, well... hmmm... where did you see that coupon? Trust me when I tell you that organization is key when it comes to couponing!

Now, there are a few methods that seem to really get the job done in coupon organization. You will have to decide which works best for you and your shopping style. Here are the two that the Couponing Divas use and recommend!

Organize by Category

* Any 2 inch, 3-ring binder will get you started, but it is a good idea to either have a zippered closure or a hard cover at minimum. You will not want to use a flimsy binder.

* Get yourself two packs (or 60 pages) of Baseball card holders as they have 9 slots on each page and work best to hold all of your clipped coupons. You can get these at Toys r' us, Target, Wal-mart, or any other store that sells baseball card memorabilia. You will need to begin with at least two packages or 60 pages.

* To separate your binder into categories you will want to get dividers with tabs, 25-30 tabs should do it.

* Next, you will want to think about in what order will make more sense for you to put your coupons in your

binder. I have included a list of the most common categories but as you set up your binder you may think of other categories that you would like to add. This particular list is in alphabetical order for your convenience; however you are going to want to place them in your binder in the order that best works for you. I find for me that it works best to put all the grocery coupons in the front. I place the categories in the order that I normally shop. This way I can just flip through each page as I go through the store in the event that I missed a deal or find a clearance item I was unaware of. I also do this so that when I make my shopping list, my brain and my book follow the same path. I place the "drug store" type items next, followed by miscellaneous and restaurant coupons. You might find that you prefer alphabetical order or divided by ingredients that go with particular meal preparation.

Air Fresheners/Candles
Baby
Baking & Candy
Beauty
Canned Goods
Cereal & Breakfast
Cleaners
Condiments
Dairy
Drinks
Freezer
Fruit
Granola Bars/Fruit Snacks
Hair Care
Hygiene
Lotion
Miscellaneous
Paper Products
Pasta & Rice
Pets
Pharmacy
Produce
Restaurant
Sides
Vegetables

Print this list and cut out each label to fit into the divider tabs. If you need to add an item you can do so by using a program like Microsoft Works Word Processor or Microsoft Office.

* Now your binder is ready for coupons! See "tips on cutting your coupon clipping time in half" at the end of this chapter.

* Make sure that when you are putting your coupons into the baseball card holders, you place them so you can easily read the expiration date.

It is very time consuming when you first set up your coupon binder don't let that discourage you, it is all worth it in the long run. It also becomes easier as you use your binder system each week and learn by sight where everything goes.

Make it a family event!

If you have kids, let them help out. Not only does it alleviate you from having to do all of the clipping, sorting and filing alone but it will also be a great opportunity to teach them the value of coupons and saving for their future. I get a little sick to my stomach when I think about all the money I have potentially thrown away over the years. I wish my mother would have taught me this great skill when I was younger. College days might have seemed less bleak in the hunger department! Ah, to have known then what I know now.

Organize by Date

* This method works well if you like to use a file system and do not mind taking extra time to compile your shopping list and coupons for each shopping trip.

* You will need a plastic file box. You should consider one with a closeable lid so that in the event that it gets knocked over, your coupons will not

end up in a heap of a mess.

* Use hanging files with tabs.

* Most coupons are issued in the Sunday paper. On the top of each set of coupon inserts, write the date they were issued.

* Use an Excel type program or Word program to make a master list of the coupons included in the insert, the amount of each and the expiration date.

* Label the hanging file tab with the same date and drop the inserts into the slot with the master list towards the front of the file. This will come in handy when putting your shopping list together and will avoid having to search through each insert every time you shop. When you see a coupon you need listed, pull out that insert and clip it.

Tips on cutting your coupon clipping time in half!

I am sure there are many methods out there to achieve the same goal. However, for myself, I like to make the most of my couponing. I do not want to spend all day clipping coupons and when you are getting 10 newspapers, each with 100 coupons that is 1000 coupons each Sunday to clip! Sound exhausting? It can be, but not if you use the method below. You may find another system that works for you, but this may help get you started!

* Tear each of the inserts so they are in single pages.

* Be careful not to ruin the barcodes.

* If you have followed the advice in this book, you have multiple copies of each insert.

* On a large surface, spread one entire insert out in the order you tore them.

* Take another of the same inserts and tear it apart as you did the first one. Stack identical pages on top of one

another.

* Then staple them together in stacks of 10. (This makes it easier when cutting)

Coupon Clipping Tips

If you are organizing by category, clip the multiple coupons in the stacks and file them into the baseball card slot under the appropriate category.

If you are organizing by date, you will want to write the date on top of each stapled set before filing it away. If you like the idea of the binder but prefer to file by date, you can use the same type system in the binder format. Instead of using baseball card holders, you will use an 8 1/2 x 11 clear plastic protector. This may get expensive though.

Chapter 7

On the Hunt for a Deal

You are now caught up to speed on the lingo, where to get your coupons, obtaining the store policies and how to stay organized. Whew! Exhausting, isn't it? Next on the list, the juicy details on how to find the deals and put those coupons to good use!

The biggest part of this next process is going to be the "adjustment period" so to speak. It is easy to follow simple steps to get coupons and organize them for easy use, but now you have to think like a couponer in order for this entire process to really work. This is huge in how your couponing future turns out. If you are sitting there thinking that you will just use the coupons and shop as you normally do, you will never see the amount of savings that is possible. You cannot shop spur of the moment anymore. Running out to grab *just one thing* will soon be a past time. You may have to get used to shopping when the coupon stars line up vs when you decide you want to purchase a particular item.

Change the way you shop

This may very well be the most challenging task in learning to coupon. It is easy to learn something new, but it is very difficult to unlearn a habit or behavior that you have had for many years. No matter how difficult this may be, you will need to forget everything you think you know about shopping with coupons in order to be a successful couponer. The reasoning behind this is if you are going to continue to do things as you always have, you are closing your mind to learning anything new. You cannot keep doing things in the same way and expect to get different results from it. Besides, the whole reason you are reading this book is either because you are looking to learn something new to you or you have tried couponing before and did not get the results you were aiming for. The system works, you have to be open and willing to use it.

Negative thoughts breed negative results!

On occasion someone will say to me that they feel like they are stealing if they leave the store with items they did pay for. I explain to them that with coupons you *are* paying for the groceries. The difference is some people pay with dollar bills and couponers pay with paper. In actuality, they are both forms of paper, just different colors!

Do not let someone put negative thoughts in your head. There will always be someone trying to talk you out of doing the things that they themselves do not understand. Here is a perfect example of what I mean! Just a few days ago I had someone tell me that "just because you *can* get items for free does not mean you *should*!" WHAT? When I asked for an explanation her answer was that she thought the increase in the prices of groceries was a result of the use of so many people using coupons. She was convinced that the "paying" customers end up spending more to make up the difference. Let me clear something up. If anything, couponers are *helping* the retailers. As stated on many coupons, retailers who accept coupons benefit because the manufacturer reimburses them the face value of the coupon plus an additional eight cents per coupon for handling.

Fun Fact:
In the year 1965, half of all Americans were using coupons to save on their groceries.

Store Coupons

These are coupons that are issued by and for use in a specific store. You can normally find these coupons in the stores weekly sales ad. Some stores such as Walgreens, publish a monthly coupon booklet that is available at the stores entrance. Use these in conjunction with your manufacturer coupons to maximize your savings.

Manufacturer Coupon Verbiage

Manufacturer coupons have a lot of information on them. Make sure you read the fine print as this is what determines the value your coupon holds.

✴ "One coupon per item"

Rule: You may use one coupon, per item you purchase. That does not mean that you cannot use a store coupon for the same item. It only refers to the use of a manufacturer coupons only. So if you buy 10 shampoos, use one manufacturer coupon on each.

✴ "One coupon per transaction"

Rule: You may only use one coupon on one product for this purchase. You may buy multiple products, but only one coupon is valid for use.

Solution: Split your transactions up to allow for coupons. If you have three items and coupons you would buy and pay for them one at a time, splitting your shopping trip into three transactions.

✴ "One coupon per purchase, maximum 4 identical coupons in

same shopping trip"

Rule: You may buy maximum of 4 identical items and use a coupon on each one. If you want to buy more items and use coupons on them, use the solution listed above on splitting your transaction.

Here is something you can laugh at! When I first started making my way through all of the lingo and meanings of the uses or limitations of manufacturer coupons, I completely misunderstood the meaning of "per purchase" and "per transaction." For some reason, I was convinced that if you exceeded the maximum allowed that you had to either go to another store or come back on another day. I was oblivious to the fact that you could overcome this obstacle if you simply split your transactions up in the same shopping trip. So, here I was constantly crossing town running from store to store with my kids, hoping to get to my next destination before another couponer cleaned the shelf! So many times I would miss out on the deal because of that! I would get so frustrated, only to now know that I created the problem myself because I did not properly understand the verbiage. So take your time when compiling your shopping list and matching your coupons. Don't misread or misunderstand something because it could make you look silly!

Use coupons on the smallest product allowed

Many people get confused as to which product to buy with their coupons, the larger or the smaller. In fact, it is better to use the coupon on the smallest product allowed. Check the coupon to determine what that sizes are allowed. Sometimes the coupons will specify that it is "not valid on trial sizes" and others will specify "any size."

Overage Example:
XYZ Detergent... Trial size .99 cents...
XYZ Detergent has a $2.00 coupon.

$0.99
$2.00
-$1.01

The store OWES you $1.01 for each one. This is why I stress the importance of having multiple coupons. The more coupons you have, the more overages you can apply to other items.

★ If you have 50 identical coupons, you pick up 50 trial size detergents for FREE and have $50.50 to apply towards your other items. It is much better to be paid to do 50 loads of laundry, than buying the $10 bottle and save $2, costing you $8 for the same 50 loads!

★ Now, let's say you don't use XYZ Detergent, donate it to a homeless shelter or to an organization. You help someone else and get paid $50.50 to do it! This is yet another reason why you never throw away coupons for things you think you will never buy.

Making your List

Most people make their shopping list based on what items they need for the week. Savvy couponers make their list based on what sales are going on, what coupons they have and which items they can get for as close to *free* as possible.

The idea is to slowly build your stockpile to where if you need something, you have it. You are buying in advance at the best prices available. Chances are the minute you run out of razors or soap and you need to buy them, there either wont be a great sale or coupon. You want to buy when it is a BOGO or clearance or when there is a store coupon you can stack with a manufacturer on the sale item. You then use 50 coupons or more and stock up at rock bottom prices for the entire year. Then, the next time you need it, you have it. The next time you buy it will not be for a VERY long time and you wont be doing it last minute.

* Make a list of all of the items you use on a regular basis. Mark which ones are not perishable, or can be frozen.

Then start searching for deals to stock
up on these items.

Find the deals

★ You will need copies of all of the most
current sales ads for the stores in
which you shop.

★ Go through the ads and try and locate
any store coupons that you may be
able to "stack" with a manufacturer
coupon. Then look through your
coupon binder or file and try to match
any manufacturer coupons.

★ If you do not have any manufacturer
coupons do a search on one or more of
the internet sites provided or do an
internet search to see if you can locate
a printable.

★ Mark all of the BOGO deals and locate
those coupons. I try to stick to BOGO
items because in my state they do not

allow coupon doubling. The BOGO deals guarantee you to a minimum of 50% savings before you even put any coupons on them.

This is when you want to take a look at all of your coupon sites and blogs for the best deals in your area. This will save you a lot of time! Note any decent deals you come across and start gathering your coupons!

* Make sure you count your coupons twice and note on your shopping list the quantity you are buying, as well as the size you are to purchase. I recommend using an excel type program so if you have a long list of items it will be easily readable with little effort.

* If you are using an excel type program, take the extra time to also include the amount of the item, minus the coupons. This will give you a total of how much you expect to save and or spend. At the end of your transaction you will easily be able to see that all the coupons were accepted or if

something is off.

It is better to over document than under document. It may seem tedious in the beginning but the minute you need that information and don't have it, you will understand! Organization is key!

Stockpiling

Items that will not expire quickly and have a long shelf life are great stockpile items. The best items to stockpile are those you can get at a deep discount, either on clearance or a BOGO sale. In order to stockpile anything, you need to have many duplicates of identical coupons.

As an example, if you are looking to stockpile paper towels for the year and you see there is a sale on XYZ towels for $2.50 and is BOGO. There is a store coupon for $1.00 off as well as a manufacturer coupon for $1.00 off.

Stockpile Example:
XYZ Towels on sale 2 for $2.50

You are going to use one store and one manufacturer coupon on each item purchased the free items as well.

$2.50 (sale)
-$2.00 (2- $1 Store Coupons)
-$2.00 (2- $1 Manufacturer Coupon)
$0.50 for 2 (or $0.25 each)

Buy for the year:
52 towels
x$0.25 each
$13.00

That is a steal! These are the deals you are looking for! If you r store doubles coupons, your total will be much less.

You will find your own techniques, tips and tricks however the basis of couponing remains the same. It seems like a lot to grasp in the beginning, but you will soon get the hang of this and eventually get a system going and you will look forward to!

Chapter 8

Now you are thinking like a couponer!

I want to personally thank you for taking the time to read the *Couponing Divas Beginners Guide: Think like a Couponer & Shop like one too!*

You now have been flooded with all of the knowledge that I wish I had when I started out on my coupon journey. I know this book does not cover everything there is to couponing, but it gives you the basics to get you out there saving immediately.

You should now know how to locate coupons effectively, organize them so you don't miss out on a sale, locate the best scenarios for stockpiling and hunt for the best deals. Now you need to put these skills to work and start raking in the savings! This is one of those things where practice makes perfect. As each week comes and goes and you begin to really understand this new way of shopping it will all start to happen without even thinking about it. Eventually you will just start spotting deals everywhere without even looking because your thought process will be re-programmed in a sense, to think like a couponer ultimately allowing you to save 50%-70% each time you shop.

Keep in mind that it will take you about 12 weeks to build up a vast array of coupons. Don't lose focus on the goal of getting as many identical coupons as you can so you can buy in larger quantity at greater savings. However, if you go out shopping the first few times and only save $15 or $20, that is normal because you are just beginning. However, by the 6th or 7th week you should begin to notice a substantial savings if you really do your due diligence and go in with the mindset that you are buying what you ultimately need, not necessarily what you are going to use up right now.

Good luck to you in your new couponing journey! I wish you the greatest success!

Pay with Paper Challenge!

When you began reading this book, you came in with a mindset that was trained to think about spending. Now, I hope your brain has been transformed how to think like a saver. Even if you have the money to pay full price for something, would you if you don't have to?

This is my personal challenge to you. Over the next 60 days I want you to apply the information you learned in this book and track how much you are spending vs. how much you are saving. I encourage you to take your couponing journey to the next level.

Short Term:
* Make a game out of your shopping trips. Set a goal of a dollar amount or a percentage to save on a particular shopping trip. Do everything you can to stay in line with that goal. Next shopping trip, try to beat it!

Long Term:
* Set an ultimate goal to work towards.

What is something you have needed to get done or would like to do? Could you use some extra money to pay bills or maybe to go on a family vacation? Now write that goal down on a piece of paper and place it on the inside of your coupon binder so that each time you get ready to go on a shopping venture you will remember to stick to the plan. Save, save, save!

Don't buy anything you do not have a coupon for. Chances are you will get one for it soon, so wait. You have to be patient for certain deals when *paying with paper*. At the end of your shopping trip, take the amount of money listed as your savings for the day and put it aside to fund your "goal". The idea behind the concept is to pretend you are paying full price and divert that extra cash somewhere else more enjoyable.

Personal Challenge Tracking Sheet

List your Ultimate Goal here:

_____

Begin Date: _____ (Now count 60 days from this date)
End Date: _____ (the day you will finalize your totals)

* Print out this page and keep it in your coupon binder or file.
* Staple an envelope to the back of this sheet.
* Keep all receipts over the next 60 days in this envelope to track progress. Use a second envelope, label it "Savings" to keep your money in and put it in a safe place.
* At the end of each shopping trip, locate the "savings" total on your receipt. Take this amount of money and put it in the envelope labeled "Savings".
* Once you reach day 60, add up the total saving from each receipt in the envelope secured to this page. Also add up the money in the envelope labeled "savings" and enter that

amount here _____! These totals should match.

You should now have either met your goal or have a substantial savings towards your goal! Make sure to empty out your envelopes and start the process again. You do not have to limit yourself to 60 day's; you can do it for the entire year if you choose. The possibilities are endless. If you save an average of $100 per week x 52 weeks in a year, that is $5200 more than you had last year! I am sure you can find something to do with all of that extra cash!

Did you take the challenge?
Did you meet your goal?
How much did you save?
What did you do with the extra money?
Do you plan on doing it again?
Send an email to
AlwaysPayWithPaper@Gmail.com